NATIONAL GEOGRAPHIC

Keeping Clean

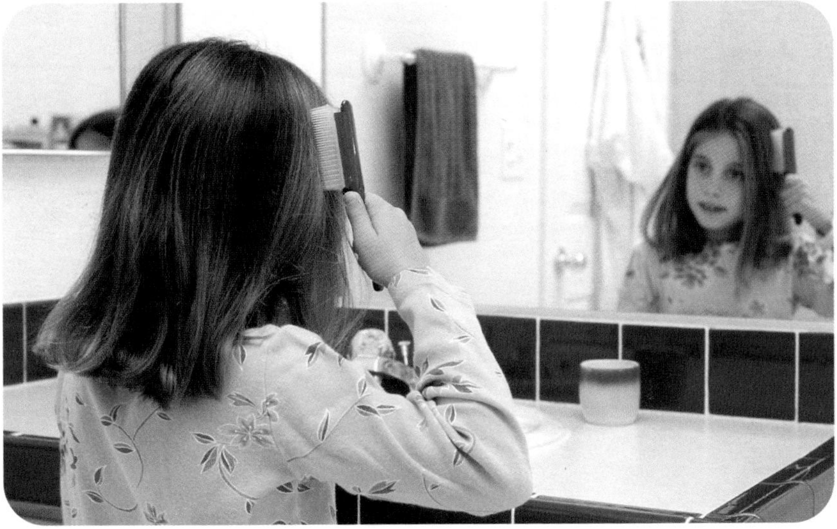

Liam Collins

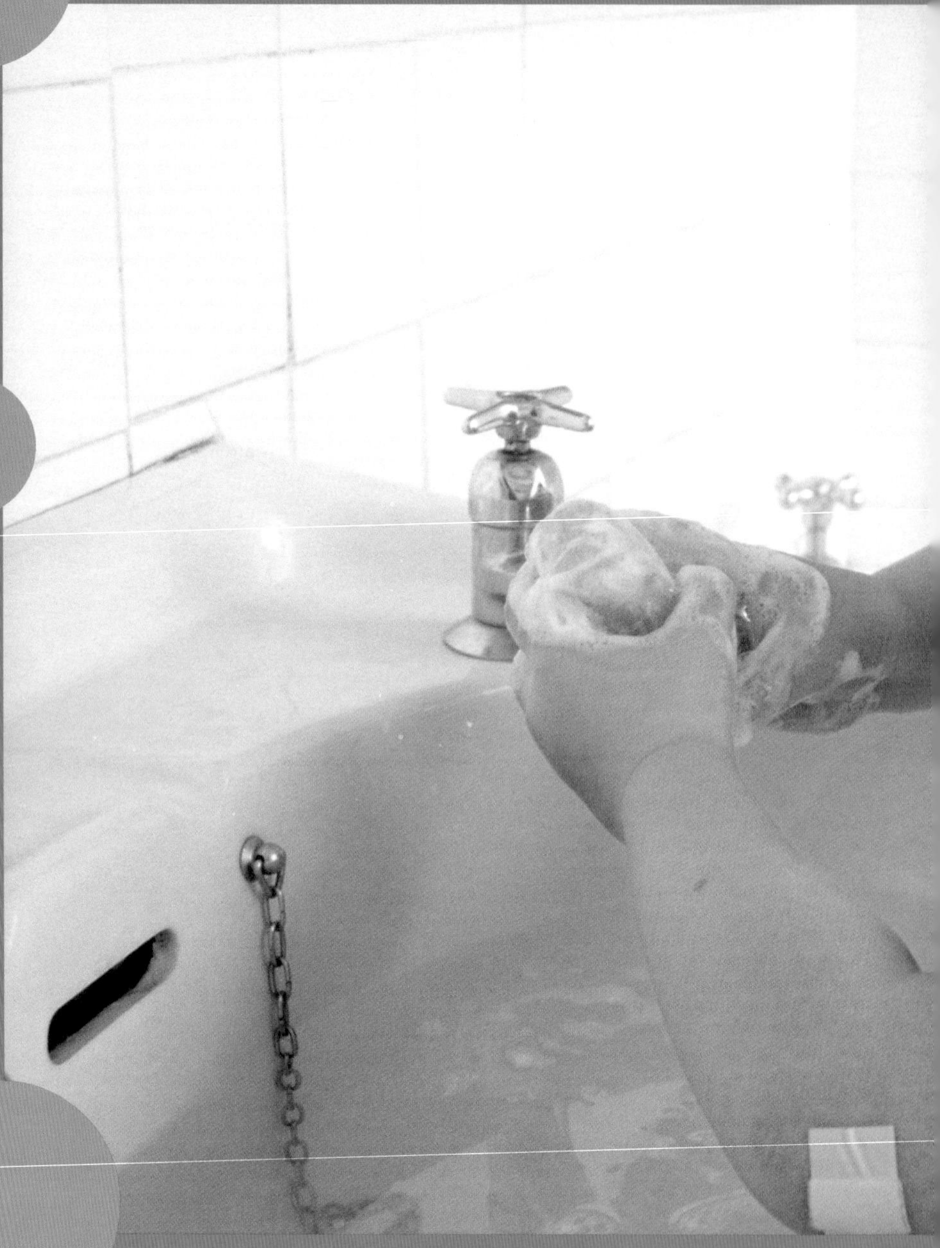

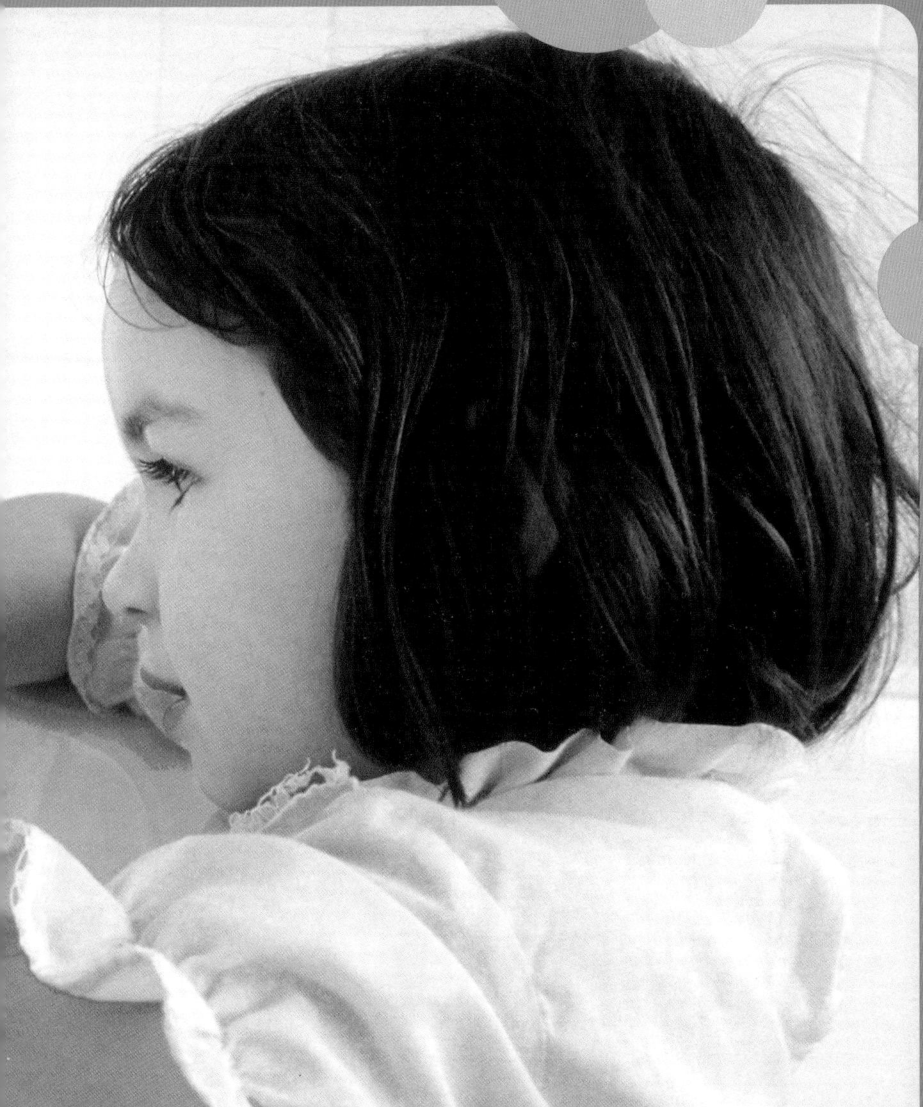

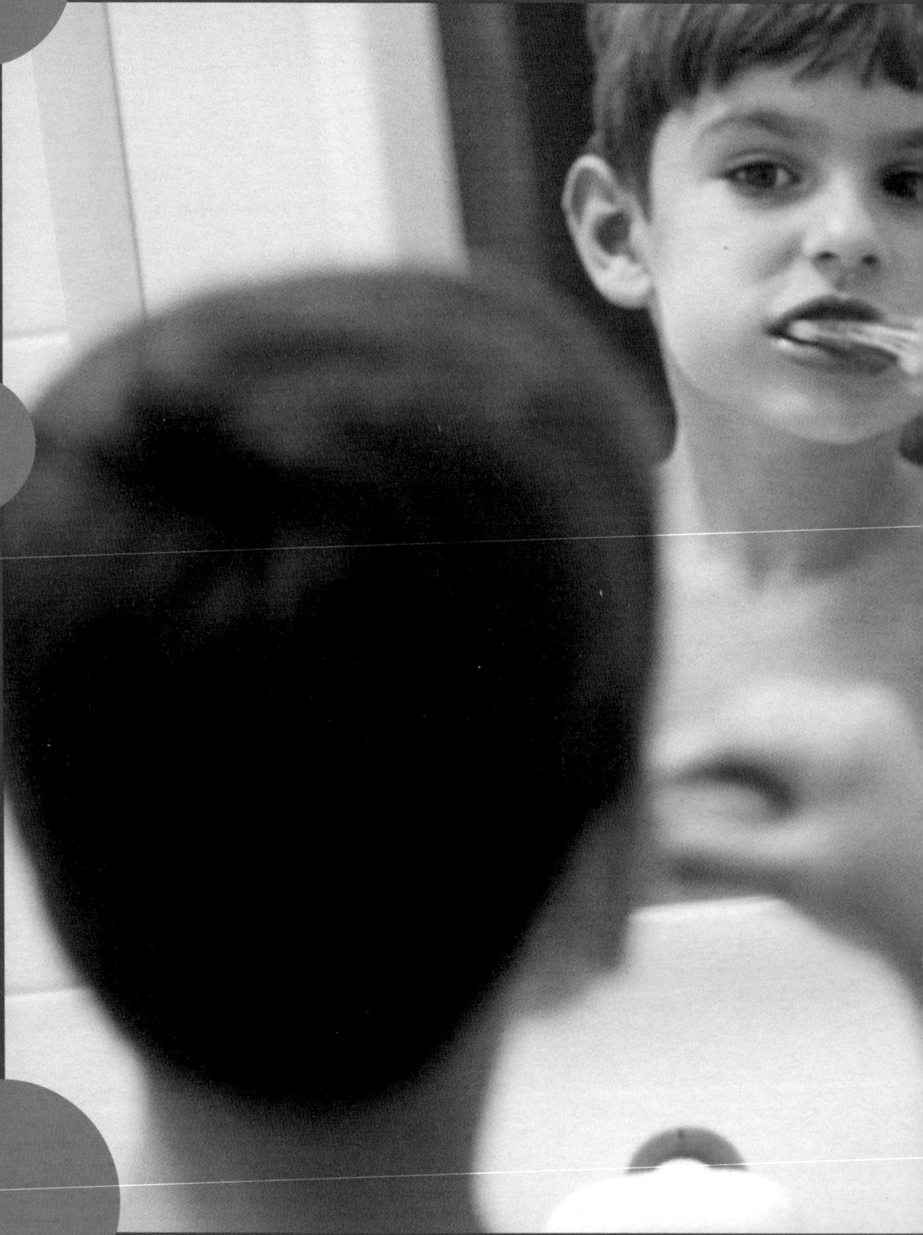

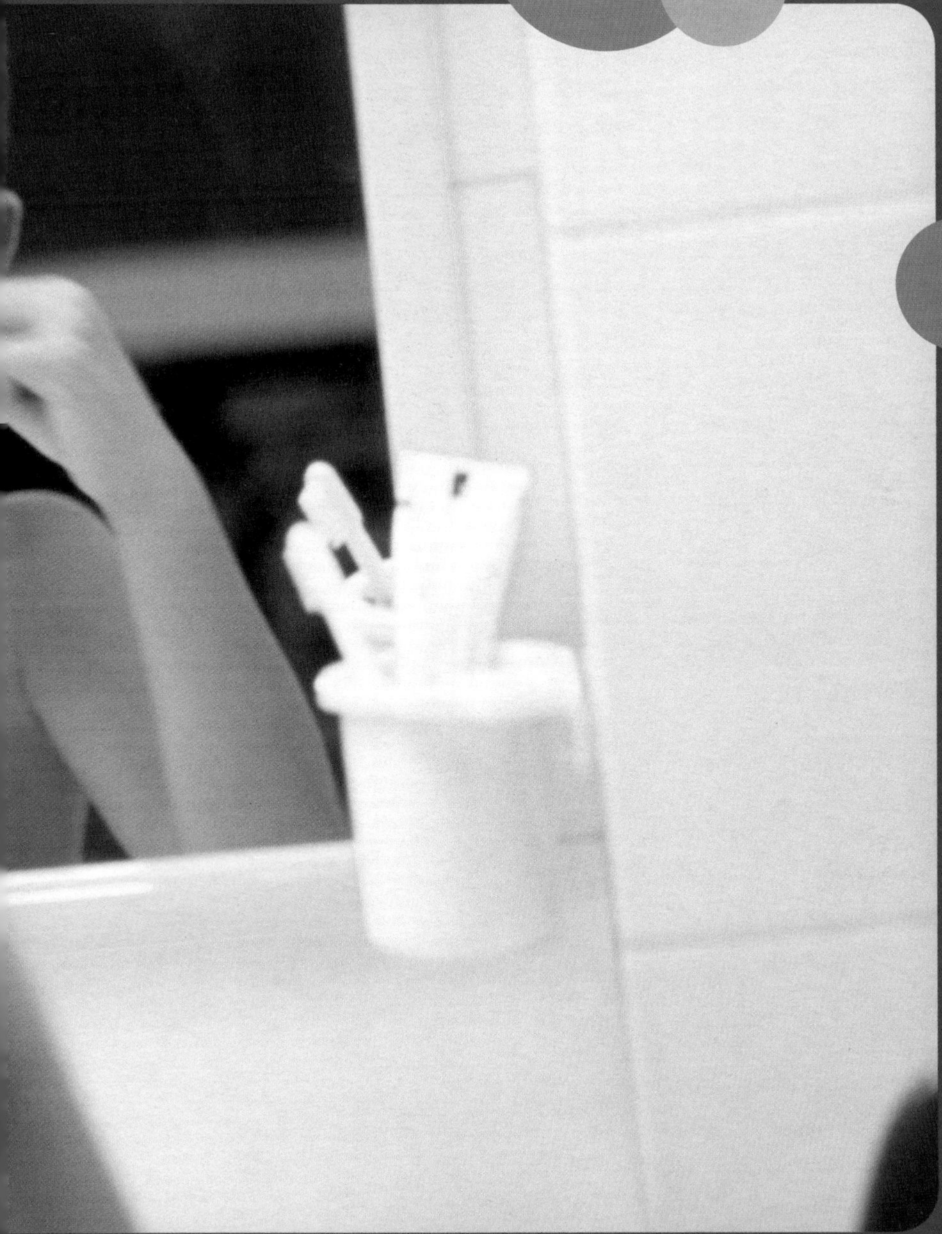

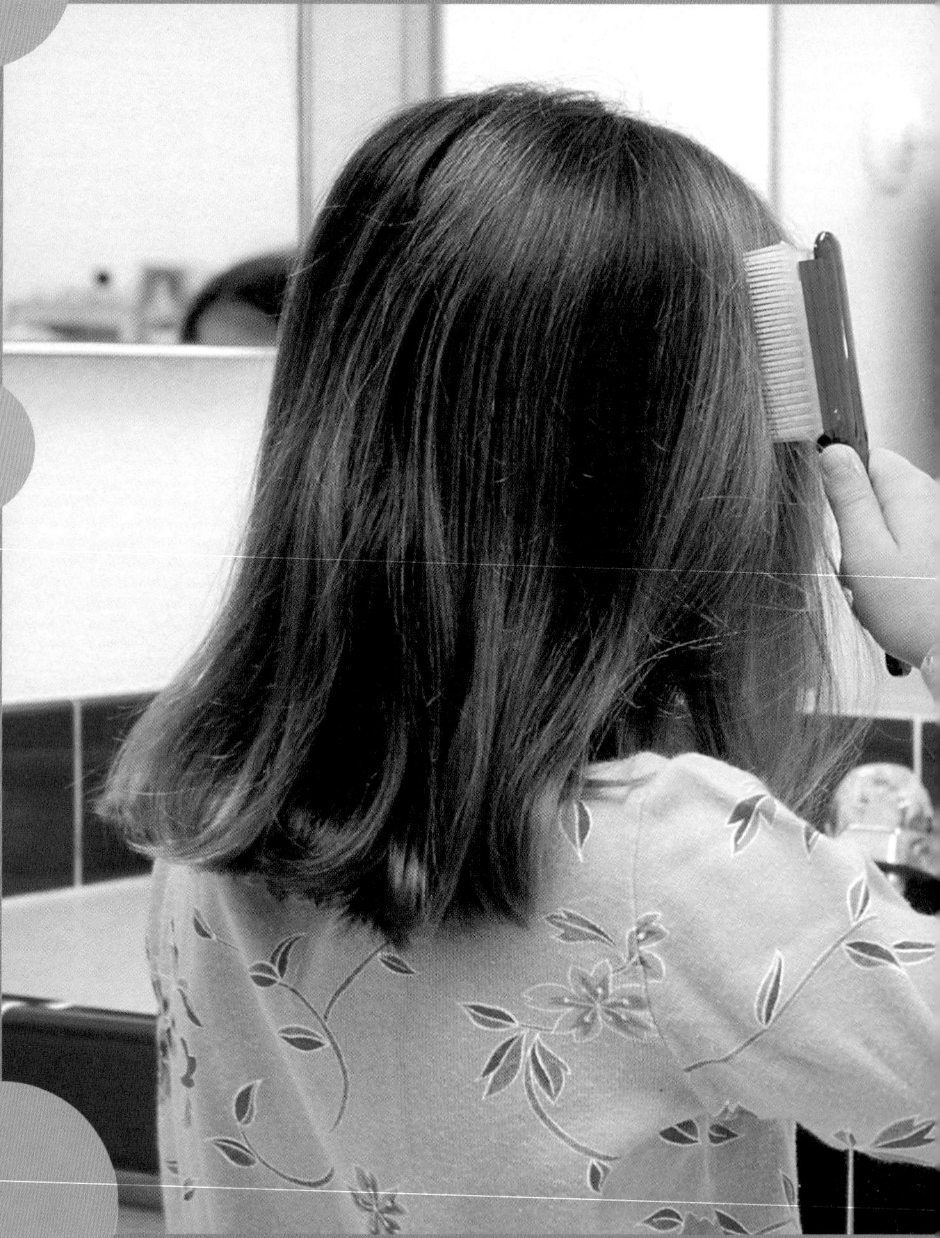

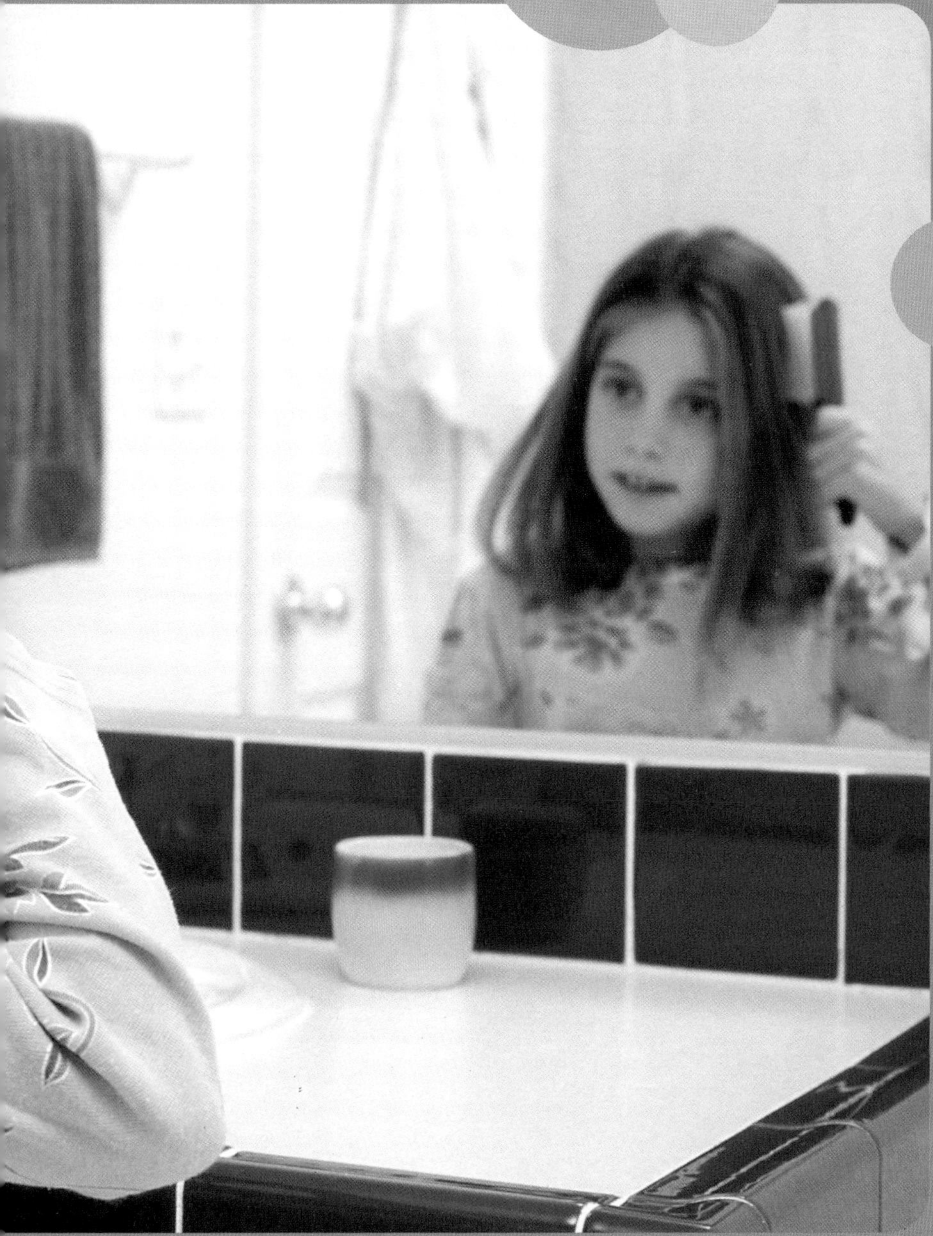

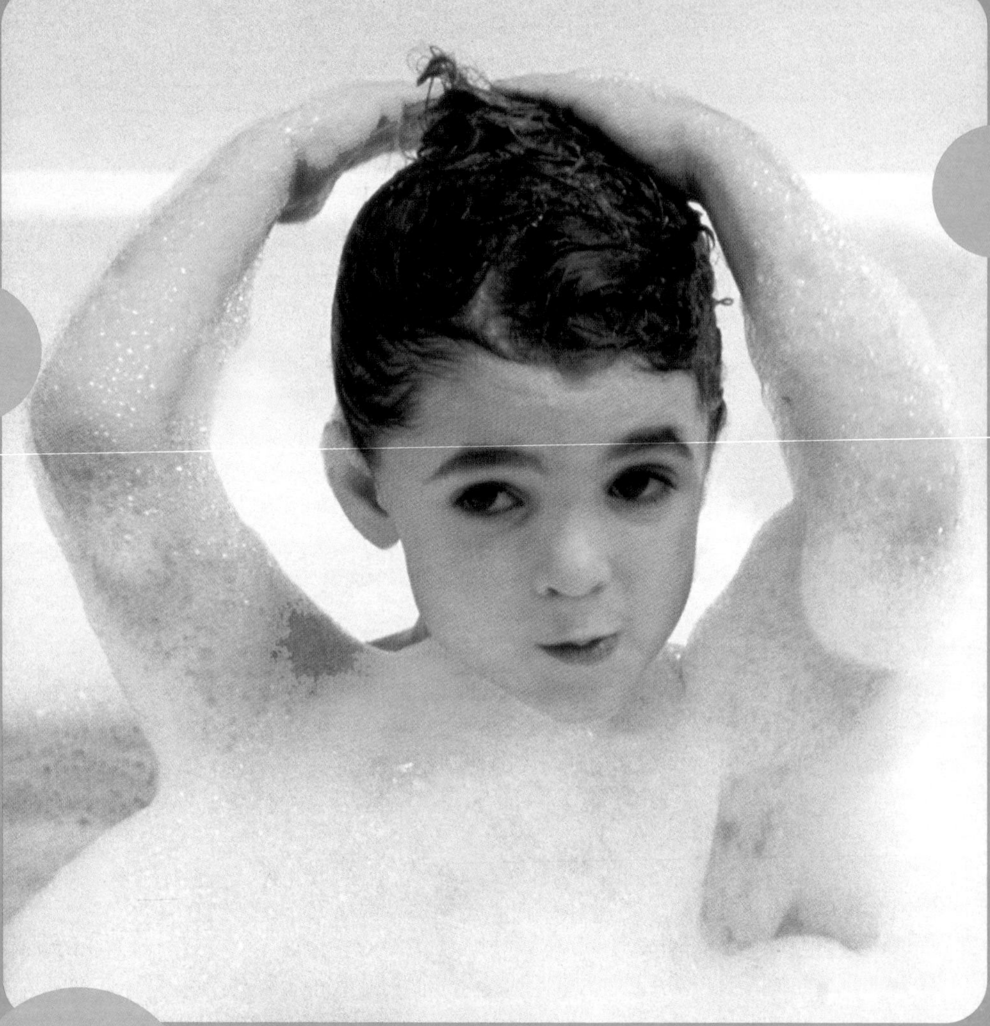